D1648250

DATE DUE

THE LITTLE BOOK

OF SHOCKING

GLOBAL FACTS

CONTENTS

[INTRODUCTION]

nternational trade has been taking place for centuries, from the Silk Road to the East India Company of the 17th century, but in the last thirty years the process has accelerated exponentially. We think nothing of wearing Brazilian flip-flops or drinking Ethiopian coffee, but is globalisation a good thing? No one could argue against the benefits of global trade, in China alone 400 million people have been lifted out of dire poverty as a result of a highly dynamic economy; but China is now the world's largest polluter, opening a new coal fired power station every week. The resulting social and cultural integration brought about through globalisation can foster broader understanding and co-operation between nations, but is it really that simple? Many developing countries suffer even more as a result of unfair trade agreements and forced liberalisation. What is the reality of globalisation and what effect does it have on each society? Who is setting the agenda, who is benefiting, who is losing out, is there such a thing as fair trade?

Furthermore the Internet has sparked a globalisation of culture and ideas. Since its birth at CERN in 1991 the World Wide Web has transformed our access to information and each other. With this in mind, this book has been designed so that certain facts connect to other parts of the book via a series of nodes and links. This in turn mirrors the interconnected nature of global trade, the fight for resources, war and human rights abuses.

01

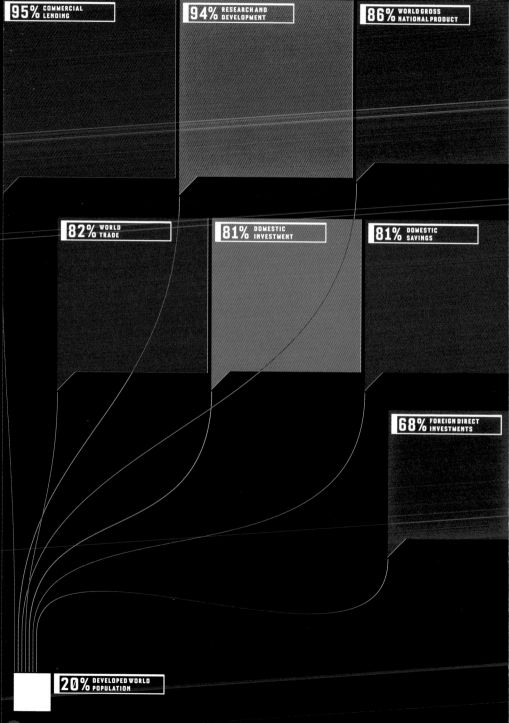

95% COMMERCIAL LENDING

94% RESEARCH AND DEVELOPMENT

86% WORLD GROSS NATIONAL PRODUCT

82% WORLD TRADE

81% DOMESTIC INVESTMENT

81% DOMESTIC SAVINGS

68% FOREIGN DIRECT INVESTMENTS

20% DEVELOPED WORLD POPULATION

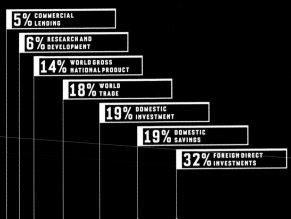

5% COMMERCIAL LENDING

6% RESEARCH AND DEVELOPMENT

14% WORLD GROSS NATIONAL PRODUCT

18% WORLD TRADE

19% DOMESTIC INVESTMENT

19% DOMESTIC SAVINGS

32% FOREIGN DIRECT INVESTMENTS

80% DEVELOPING WORLD POPULATION

WORLD WEALTH INEQUALITY

The distribution of wealth throughout the world is desperately unbalanced, with the richest two percent owning more than half of all global assets. Almost every indicator of wealth shows that the richest twenty percent of the global population control almost all of the world's resources. The situation is not improving for developing nations, as their progress is hindered by inequalities in international trade.

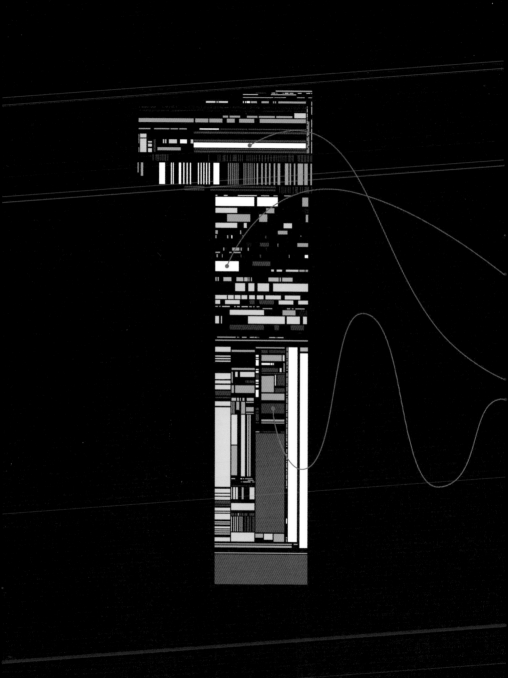

World Trade is a source of enormous wealth, yet millions of people throughout the world are losing out through unfair trade agreements and disproportionate tariffs.

If the continents of Africa, East Asia, South Asia and Latin America were able to each increase their share of world exports by just one percent, 128 million people would be lifted out of poverty. It would generate $70 billion for Africa alone; five times what it receives in aid.

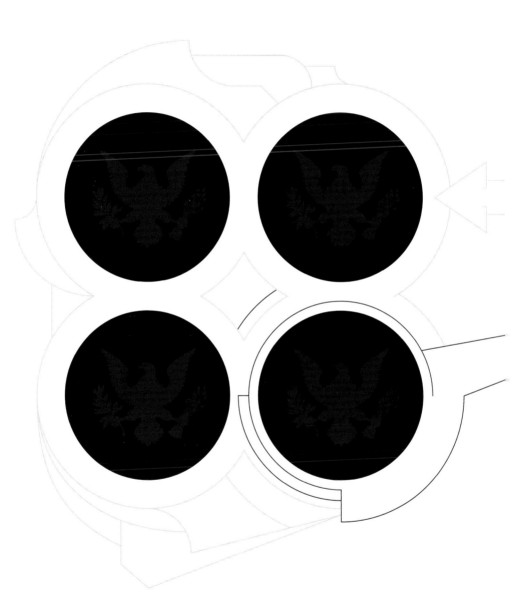

FOR EVERY **four dollars** **OF AID** **PROVIDED TO** **LESS ECONOMICALLY DEVELOPED NATIONS,** **THE MAJOR INDUSTRIALISED countries TAKE BACK one dollar through the IMPOSITION of TRADE RESTRICTIONS.**

Kenya is a prime example of the effect that excessive liberalisation can have on a country. In the 1980s Kenya was de-developed through a series of imposed trade reforms in return for aid. In the 1990s the problem was exacerbated when Kenya was forced to liberalise even further as a condition of joining the WTO. Tariffs were cut, markets de-regulated and cheap, often subsidised goods flooded the market. This has been highlighted in Kenya's once thriving cotton industry where, after liberalisation, 70,000 jobs were lost and production is now at 20% of the 1980s level.

$15,500,000

Shell, the world's second largest oil company has been working in the Niger Delta, Nigeria since 1956. During this time there have been over 4,000 oil spills and over 1,000 lawsuits lodged against the Anglo-Dutch multinational. In one of the most notorious cases, Shell was accused by activists of being complicit in murder, torture and human rights abuses carried out by Nigeria's former military government. In 1994 nine anti-oil campaigners were executed after campaigning against pollution caused by the oil industry. Shell denied any responsibility but in 2009 paid the families of the victims $15.5m in an out-of-court settlement as part of a "process of reconciliation".

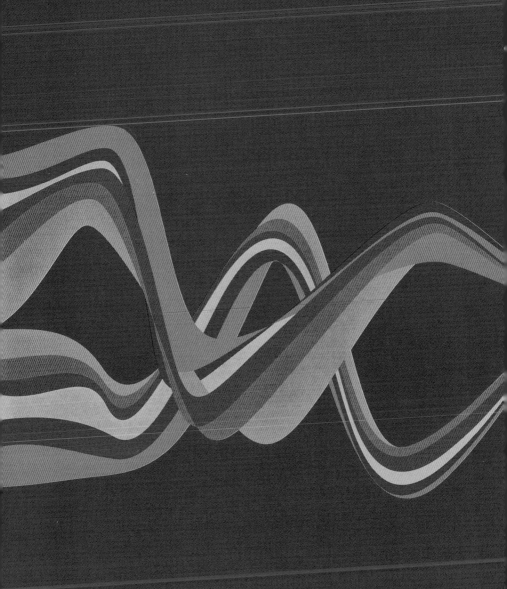

FIFTY MILLION DRIVEN INTO EXTREME POVERTY

The global financial crisis that started in 2008 slowed trade and halted investment throughout the world. The poorest countries were hit hardest, with 90 percent exposed to the impact of the crisis. As a result 50 million people were sent into extreme poverty and one hundred million into chronic hunger.

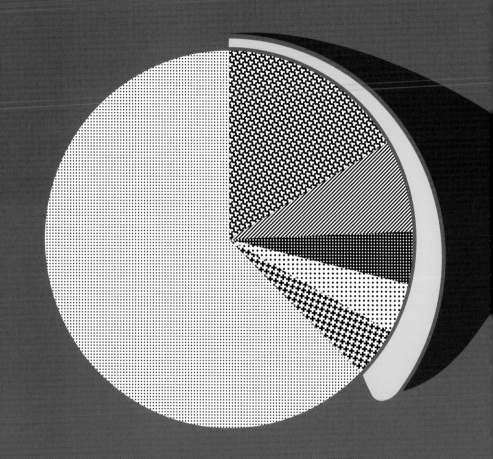

JUST FIVE COUNTRIES CONTROL OVER A THIRD OF THE WORLD BANK

Rather than one member, one vote, the World Bank is controlled by the five largest shareholding countries: the United States, Japan, Germany, France and UK. Rich nations set the agenda and loans are provided on conditions that favour those in control.

KEY

- UNITED STATES
- JAPAN
- GERMANY
- FRANCE
- UNITED KINGDOM
- REST OF THE WORLD

ollowing on from a World Bank-IMF structural
adjustment programme in 1983, Ghana's gold mining
industry has been expanded, privatised and deregulated.
Around 80% of the large scale mining is foreign owned,
and just 10% of the value stays in Ghana's economy
as mining companies repatriate their profits.
In addition to this, mining has led to the destruction
of 60% of Ghana's rainforests and the displacement
of around 50,000 indigenous people.

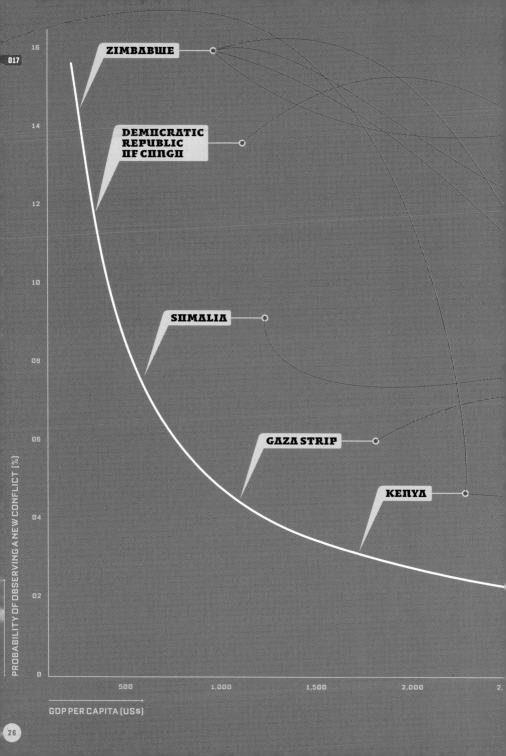

PROBABILITY OF OBSERVING A NEW CONFLICT (%)

16

14

12

10

08

06

04

02

0

ZIMBABWE

DEMOCRATIC
REPUBLIC
OF CONGO

SOMALIA

GAZA STRIP

KENYA

500   1,000   1,500   2,000   2,

GDP PER CAPITA (US$)

INCREASING WEALTH DECREASES THE POSSIBILITY OF WAR

Research by Macartan Humphreys (Columbia University) has suggested that wealth is linked to the possibility of conflict. For example, a negative economic growth shock of 5% increases the possibility of civil war by 50%. The risk of violent civil conflict decreases as wealth increases; in fact 22 of the world's 34 poorest countries are emerging from – or are engaged in – armed conflict. Notable historical examples of economies on the brink of collapse include 1930s Germany and the former Yugoslavia in the early 1990s, both of which experienced hyperinflation leading up to the outbreak of war.

3,000   3,500   4,000   4,500   5,000

231,000,000%

069

123

143

In January 2009 The Reserve Bank of Zimbabwe issued a one hundred trillion dollar note (that's fifteen zeros), less than a month after issuing a fifty trillion dollar note. Zimbabwe's economy collapsed as hyperinflation reached 231m% in July 2008. The result was a worthless currency with loaves of bread costing more than a daily withdrawal allowance.

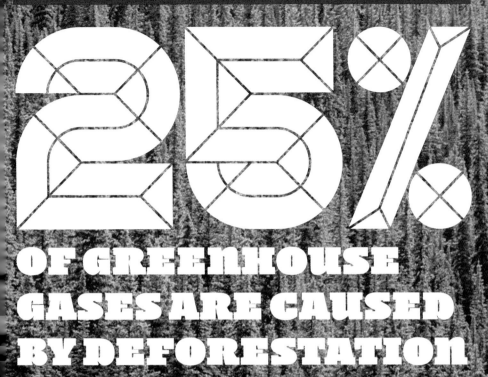

25%

OF GREENHOUSE GASES ARE CAUSED BY DEFORESTATION

15

10

05

00

-05

-10

-15

-20

-25

-30

-35

-40

-45

-50

-55

-60

-65

AREA: 1,000,000 HECTARES

037

038

073

079

099

103

111

112

120

165

The primary source of greenhouse gas emissions is not the burning of fossil fuels, but deforestation. In fact 25% of greenhouse gases released each year – 1.6 billion tonnes – are caused by the felling or burning of trees.

Deforestation occurs at a rate of 13 million hectares per year, and is mainly caused by converting forests into agricultural land. The main areas of deforestation occur in the tropics of Africa and South America. Deforestation also occurs at a high rate in Asia, but total figures are distorted by large scale afforestation reported by China. The only continent to report a positive change in forest area during the period 1990 – 2005 was Europe.

Between 1990 and 2005, Brazil cleared 42,329,000 hectares of forest – an area larger than Germany.

The main cause of Brazil's deforestation is cattle ranching. Brazil is the biggest beef exporter in the world and has the largest cattle herd on the planet, 40% of which is located within the Amazon basin. Land-use change and deforestation – which is mostly done by fire – make up 75% of all Brazil's greenhouse gas emissions.

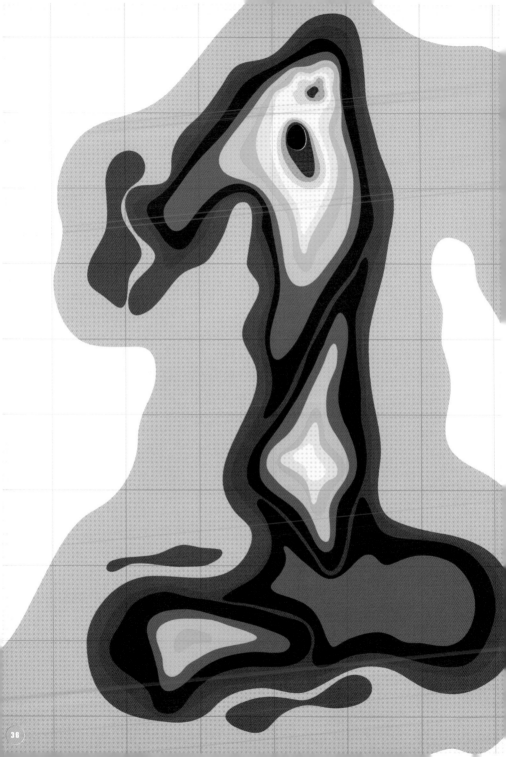

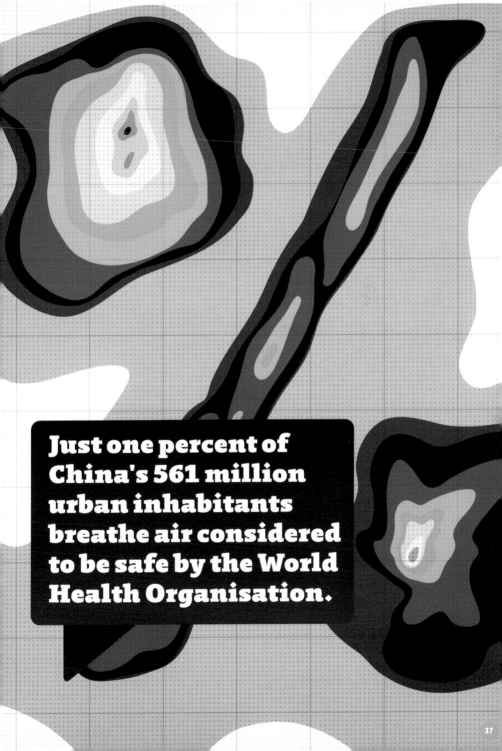

Just one percent of China's 561 million urban inhabitants breathe air considered to be safe by the World Health Organisation.

THE WORLD'S LARGEST HYDROELECTRIC PROJECT

China's Three Gorges Dam

China – the world's largest polluter – has tried to curb its dependence
on fossil fuels by building the world's largest hydroelectric power
generator. It is designed to produce more than 18,000 megawatts
of electricity – twenty times the power of the Hoover Dam.
There has been much criticism of its environmental impact,
which includes the extinction of the Baiji river dolphin; landslides;
and a decline in phytoplankton (the base of fishery food chains),
which threatens the fish population of the East China Sea.
In addition to this, 1.3 million people have been displaced
from 13 cities, 140 towns and 1,350 villages.

TOP 20 CARBON EMITTING COUNTRIES

KEY: MILLION METRIC TONS OF CARBON DIOXIDE PER YEAR

| <500 | 500–1000 | 1000–2000 | >2000 |

7. Canada

2. USA

13. Mexico

8. UK

6. Germany

15. France

18. Spain

11. Italy

17. Brazil

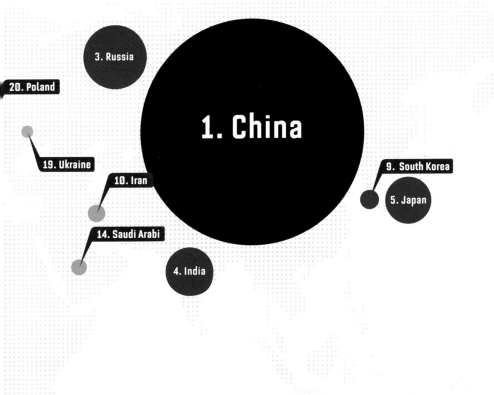

3. Russia

20. Poland

1. China

19. Ukraine

10. Iran

9. South Korea

5. Japan

14. Saudi Arabi

4. India

16. Australia

12. South Africa

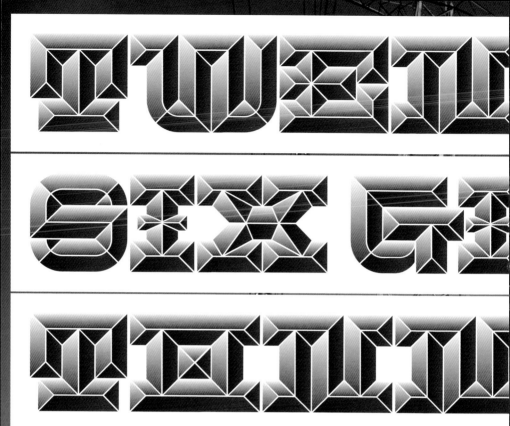

TWENTY SIX GT

The World Bank is in a unique position to finance environmentally friendly programs in the energy sector yet it continues to support large-scale fossil fuel extraction projects. A report in 2008 by WWF calculated that between 1997 and 2007, the World Bank had financed energy projects which produced more than 26 Gigatonnes of lifetime CO_2 emissions. That's about 45 times what the UK produces annually. However this does not tell the full story; the estimate given by WWF was "extremely conservative" and only concentrated on the energy sector. If other sectors such as transport were included the total would be far greater.

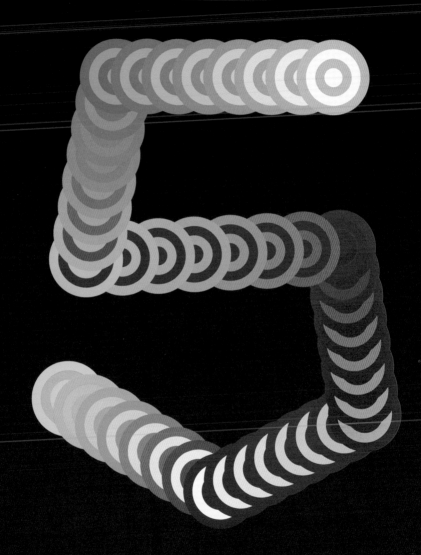

Critics suggest the UK's
push towards nuclear power will
not solve climate change. Even if ten
new nuclear reactors were built by 2024,
UK carbon emissions would be cut by just
four percent. It would simply create more
nuclear waste for future generations.
The UK could already fill the Royal
Albert Hall five times over with
its radioactive waste.

400 Times More Radioactive than Little Boy

The worst nuclear power plant disaster in history, and the only event to reach level 7 (maximum) on the InES scale occurred on 26 April 1986 at Chernobyl, Ukraine (then part of the Soviet Union). The release of radioactivity was around 400 times higher than the fallout of the atomic bomb dropped on Hiroshima. There is now a 30 kilometre exclusion zone surrounding the plant where the accident took place, creating a ghost town where over 300,000 people have abandoned their homes.

+1°C

Small glaciers in the Andes will disappear, threatening the water supplies of up to 50 million people.

+2°C

Between 40 and 60 million more people will be exposed to malaria in Africa alone.

+3°C

150–550 million more people will be at risk of hunger due to drought and lower crop yields; one to three million of whom will die each year due to malnutrition.

+4°C

Up to 300 million more people will be affected by coastal flooding each year.

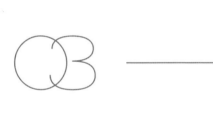

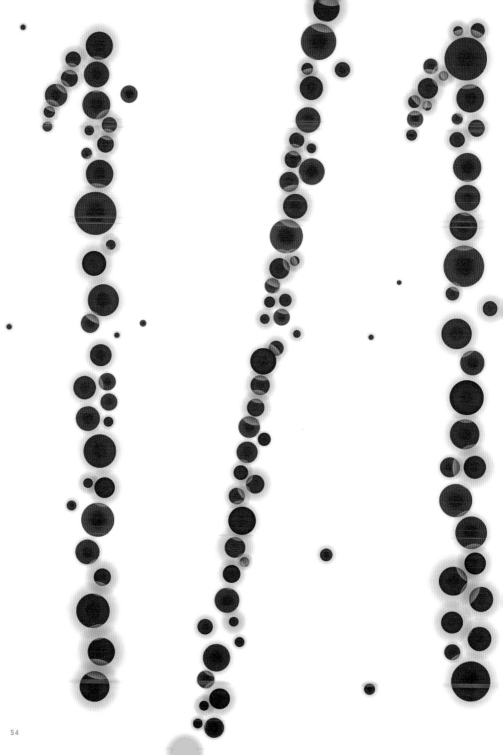

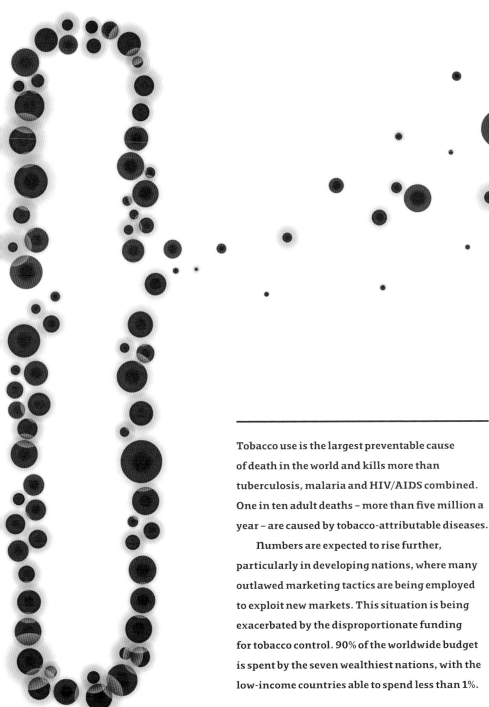

Tobacco use is the largest preventable cause of death in the world and kills more than tuberculosis, malaria and HIV/AIDS combined. One in ten adult deaths – more than five million a year – are caused by tobacco-attributable diseases.

Numbers are expected to rise further, particularly in developing nations, where many outlawed marketing tactics are being employed to exploit new markets. This situation is being exacerbated by the disproportionate funding for tobacco control. 90% of the worldwide budget is spent by the seven wealthiest nations, with the low-income countries able to spend less than 1%.

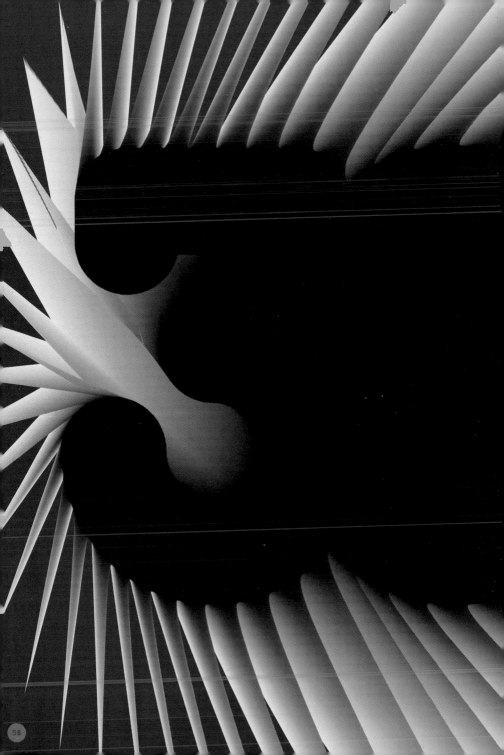

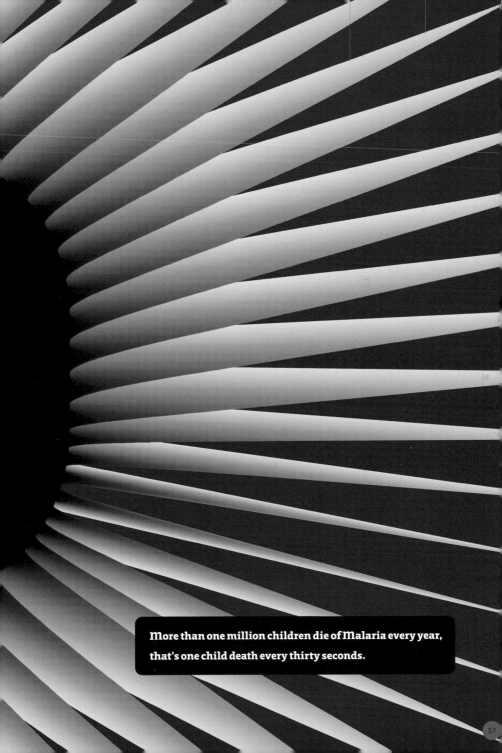

More than one million children die of Malaria every year, that's one child death every thirty seconds.

Every day 6,000
people are killed
by HIV/AIDS and
another 8,200
are infected.

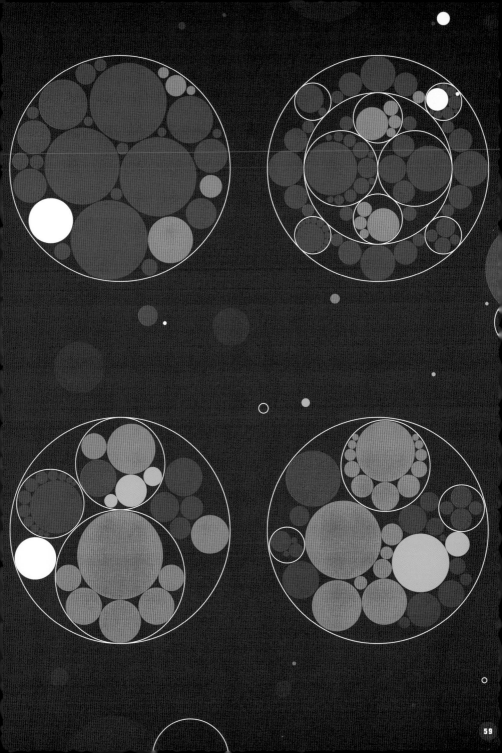

Life expectancy in Swaziland is the lowest in the world

32 YEARS

The HIV rate in Swaziland is the highest in the world

39 PERCENT

Swaziland is a small landlocked country in Southern Africa. Just twenty years after the first reported AIDS case, Swaziland is caught in the midst of an epidemic. It has the highest HIV/AIDS rate in the world, and the lowest life expectancy. The epidemic has been fuelled by high unemployment and poverty as well as conservative traditional and religious beliefs about condom use.

THE US
PHARMACEUTICAL
INDUSTRY

SPENDS

24.4%

+

ON PROMOTION

AND JUST

13.4%

+

ON RESEARCH AND
DEVELOPMENT

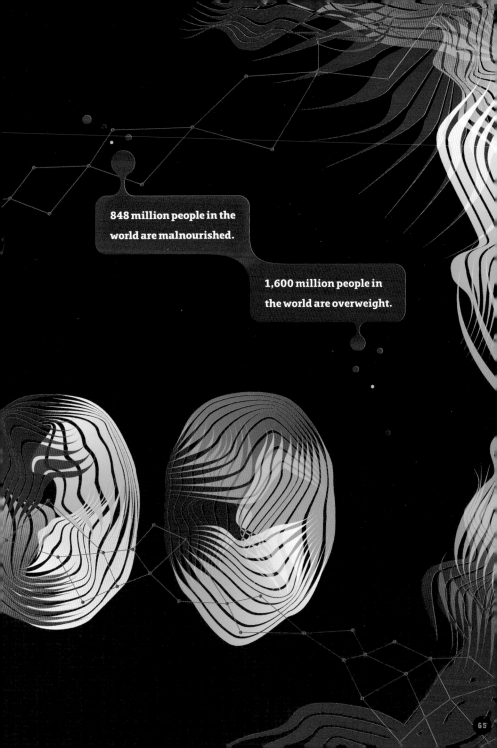

WORLD WATER FACTS

2/3 people lacking access to clean water survive on less than $2 a day.

2.6 billion people do not have basic sanitation.

one billion people use unsafe sources of drinking water

4/10 people don't have access to a simple latrine.

1/3 people lacking access to clean water survive on less than $1 a day.

50% of Africans suffer from water-related diseases.

5 times as many children die due to diarrhoea caused by unclean water than die from HIV/AIDS.

Between August 2008 and June 2009 Zimbabwe experienced a catastrophic cholera outbreak, the worst in Africa for 15 years. Over 90,000 cases – 4,000 of them fatal – occurred in less than a year. People were forced to rely on unhygienic water supplies, exacerbating the problems created by a chronic lack of basic sanitation and an incapable health system.

123

143

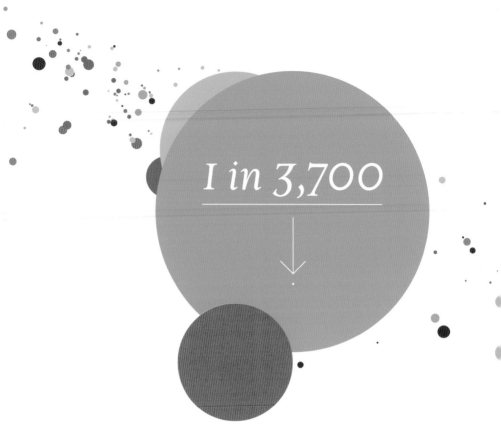

I in 3,700

I in I6

99% of all women that die in childbirth are from developing countries. The chance of dying in sub-Saharan Africa is one in sixteen, compared to a risk of 1 in 3,700 for a woman from North America.

How much for my organs?

Kidney $70,000

Pancreas $110,000

Liver $130,000

Lung $150,000

Heart $130,000

Transplant tourism is a growing phenomenon resulting from the universal lack of available organs. Patients travel (mostly from developed countries) to buy organs from donors (mostly from developing countries). Countries well known for exporting organs include India, where around 2,000 people sell kidneys every year. Other examples include China, where many organs are alleged to have been removed from executed prisoners. Some Chinese websites are also known for arranging transplant tourism over the internet, where these organ costs were offered.

079
079
099
103
106
111
112
120
165

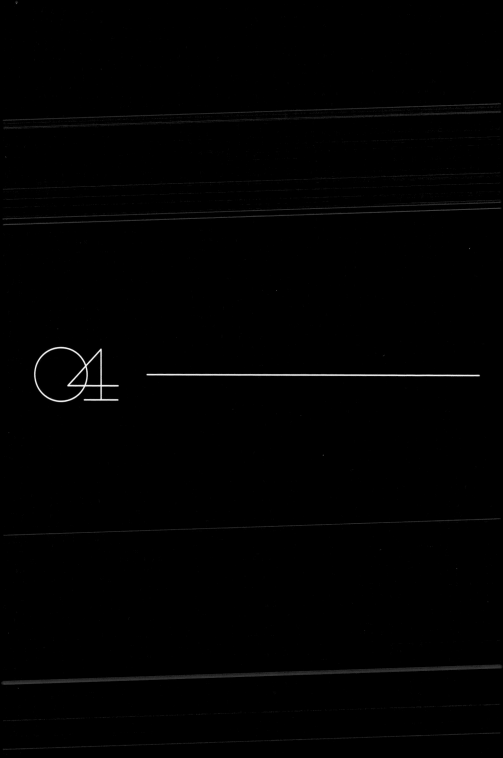

POPULATION

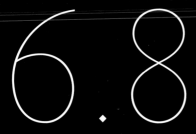

6.8

—

BILLION

PEOPLE LIVING

ON PLANET EARTH

—

THAT'S 5 BILLION PEOPLE ADDED
TO THE PLANET SINCE 1900.
THIS POPULATION GROWTH RATE
IS ONLY A RECENT PHENOMENON.
IN 1750 THE POPULATION WAS
ESTIMATED TO BE AROUND
791 MILLION. IN 150 YEARS IT
SLIGHTLY MORE THAN DOUBLED
TO 1.7 BILLION IN 1900. WE NOW
HAVE A POPULATION ALMOST
FOUR TIMES THAT FIGURE.

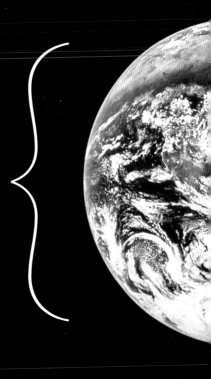

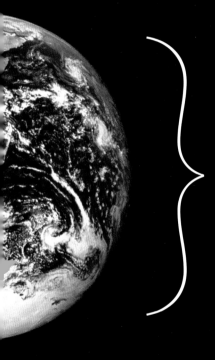

} 5.6

B I L L I O N

P E O P L E   L I V I N G   I N

L E S S   D E V E L O P E D   R E G I O N S

THAT'S 82 PERCENT OF THE
WORLD'S TOTAL. OUT OF THESE,
835 MILLION RESIDE IN THE
49 LEAST DEVELOPED COUNTRIES
AND ACCOUNT FOR 12 PERCENT
OF THE WORLD POPULATION.
MORE DEVELOPED COUNTRIES,
WHOSE TOTAL POPULATION
AMOUNTS TO 1.2 BILLION
INHABITANTS, ACCOUNT FOR 18 PER-
CENT OF THE WORLD POPULATION.

033
037
038

073
073

59.3%

(4 BILLION) OF THE GLOBAL POPULATION LIVE IN JUST TEN COUNTRIES

CHINA	19.71%
INDIA	17.54%
USA	4.61%
INDONESIA	3.37%
BRAZIL	2.84%
PAKISTAN	2.65%
BANGLADESH	2.38%
NIGERIA	2.27%
RUSSIA	2.06%
JAPAN	1.86%

40.7%

By 2025, the population of India is projected to surpass that of China. India has also experienced rapid growth of its urban population, with Mumbai projected to become the world's second biggest city by 2025.

099
103
106
111
112
120
165

HIGHEST BIRTH RATE

(51.60 BIRTHS PER 1000 PEOPLE)

NIGER

HIGHEST FERTILITY RATE

(7.75 CHILDREN BORN PER WOMAN)

13%

URBAN POPULATION IN 1900

50%

URBAN POPULATION IN 2007

In 1900, thirteen percent of the global population lived in urban areas. After a century of rapid urbanisation that figure has risen to fifty percent. This is a landmark moment in history, when the global population has moved from being mostly rural to mostly urban.

TOP 10 LARGEST URBAN AGGLOMERATIONS

YEAR		RANK	AGGLOMERATION	POPULATION (MILLIONS)
1975		1.	TOKYO	26.615
		2.	NEW YORK-NEWARK	15.880
		3.	CIUDAD DE MÉXICO (MEXICO CITY)	10.690
		4.	OSAKA-KOBE	9.844
		5.	SÃO PAULO	9.614
		6.	LOS ANGELES-LONG BEACH-SANTA ANA	8.926
		7.	BUENOS AIRES	8.745
		8.	PARIS	8.5585
		9.	KOLKATA (CALCUTTA)	7.888
		10.	MOSKVA (MOSCOW)	7.6231
2007	—	1.	TOKYO	35.676
	—	2.	NEW YORK-NEWARK	19.04035
	—	3.	CIUDAD DE MÉXICO (MEXICO CITY)	19.028
	▲	4.	MUMBAI (BOMBAY)	18.978
	—	5.	SÃO PAULO	18.845
	▲	6.	DELHI	15.926
	▲	7.	SHANGHAI	14.987
	▲	8.	KOLKATA (CALCUTTA)	14.787
	▲	9.	DHAKA	13.485
	▲	10.	BUENOS AIRES	12.795

35.676 MILLION PEOPLE

Tokyo, the capital of Japan is the most populous urban agglomeration in the world and one of 19 megacities (at least 10 million inhabitants). The Tokyo metropolitan area not only consists of Tokyo city, but 87 surrounding cities and towns, and is the most densely populated area of Japan.

SLUM POPULATION

81-100%
61-80%
41-60%
21-40%
0-20%
NO DATA

As the world's urban population increases, the immigrant poor
flock to vast, densely populated, informal settlements – slums –
to exploit the perceived economic prospects that cities can offer.
Slum households are often ramshackle structures characterised
by squalid living conditions, inadequate sanitation and poor
security. In the developed world the percentage of urban
population living in slums is non-existent. In less developed
regions the proportion is 37% and this rises still further for the least
developed regions where 74% of the urban population live in slums.
The continent of Africa is where the problem is most pronounced,
in some countries over 90% of the urban population live in slums.

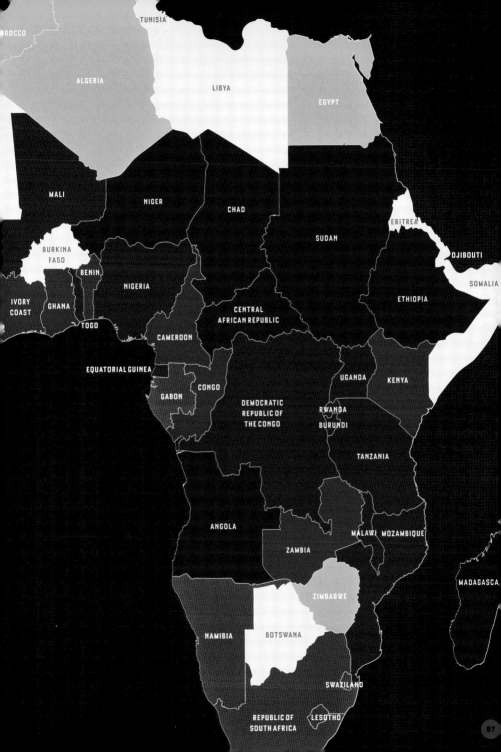

LARGEST SLUM IN THE WORLD

Kibera is the world's largest slum and houses around one million of the 2.5 million slum dwellers of Nairobi, Kenya. 60% of the Nairobi population live in slums, which take up just 6% of the land. Conditions in Kibera are grim; the average size of a mud shack is 3.5 square metres and sleeps eight people. There are few toilets – one latrine can be shared by up to 50 shacks.

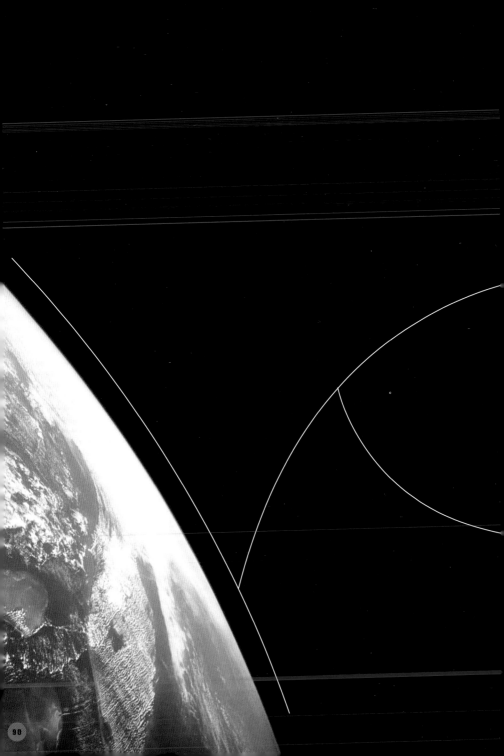

42

MILLION

FORCIBLY DISPLACED PEOPLE

In 2008, there were 42 million

forcibly displaced people worldwide.

That includes:

26 million internally displaced people

15.2 million refugees

6.6 million stateless people

827,000 asylum-seekers

are refugees
flooding
developed
countries?

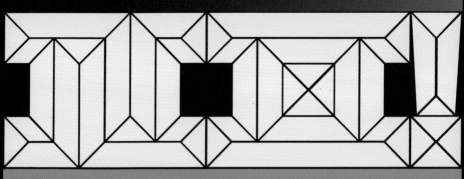

All available statistical evidence points to the fact that most refugees flee to neighbouring countries and therefore remain in their region of origin. It is estimated that only 14% of the global refugee population exist outside their region of origin.

IRAN

AFGHANISTAN'S REFUGEE CRISIS

For the last thirty years Afghanistan has been the leading country of origin for refugees and today one in four (2.8 million) originate from Afghanistan. Almost all of these (96 percent) have fled to neighbouring Pakistan and Iran, with the rest in another 69 countries worldwide. The second highest refugee population originates from Iraq; together Afghan and Iraqi refugees account for almost half of the global refugee population.

TURKMENISTAN

UZBEKISTAN

TAJIKISTAN

AFGHANISTAN

PAKISTAN

133

150
152

155
167

INDIA

95

Human
Rights

THE GLOBAL PRISON POPULATION

8.75
MILLION PEOPLE

Are held in prisons throughout the world.
Around half of these are held in just three countries:

UNITED STATES	CHINA	RUSSIA
1.96M	1.43M	0.92M

The USA also has the highest documented
per capita rate of incarceration in the world.

TOP TEN HIGHEST PRISON
POPULATION RATES

PRISONERS HELD PER 100,000
OF THE NATIONAL POPULATION

01	UNITED STATES	686
02	CAYMAN ISLANDS	664
03	RUSSIA	638
04	BELARUS	554
05	KAZAKHSTAN	522
06	TURKMENISTAN	489
07	BELIZE	459
08	BAHAMAS	447
09	SURINAME	437
10	DOMINICA	420

GUANTÁNAMO BAY
NUMBERS

800
NUMBER OF DETAINEES THAT HAVE BEEN HELD IN GUANTÁNAMO.

26
NUMBER OF DETAINEES CHARGED FOR TRIAL BY MILITARY COMMISSION.

3
NUMBER OF DETAINEES THAT HAVE BEEN CONVICTED AND SENTENCED.

6
NUMBER OF DETAINEES THAT HAVE HAD CHARGES AGAINST THEM DISMISSED.

6
NUMBER OF DETAINEES THAT ARE FACING THE DEATH PENALTY.

NUMBER OF DETAINEES REPORTED TO HAVE DIED AS A RESULT OF SUICIDE.

4

AMOUNT IN HOURS DURING THE DAY THAT DETAINEES ARE CONFINED IN INDIVIDUAL, WINDOWLESS CELLS.

22

55

PERCENT OF DETAINEES NOT DETERMINED TO HAVE COMMITTED ANY HOSTILE ACTS AGAINST THE UNITED STATES OR ITS COALITION ALLIES.

86

PERCENT OF DETAINEES ARRESTED BY PAKISTAN OR THE AFGHANISTAN-BASED NORTHERN ALLIANCE (FOR A CASH REWARD).

5

PERCENT OF DETAINEES CAPTURED BY UNITED STATES FORCES.

PERCENT OF DETAINEES CHARACTERISED AS AL-QAEDA FIGHTERS.

PERCENT OF DETAINEES WITH NO CONNECTION TO AL-QAEDA.

PERCENT OF DETAINEES WITH NO CONNECTION TO EITHER AL-QAEDA OR THE TALIBAN.

8

40

18

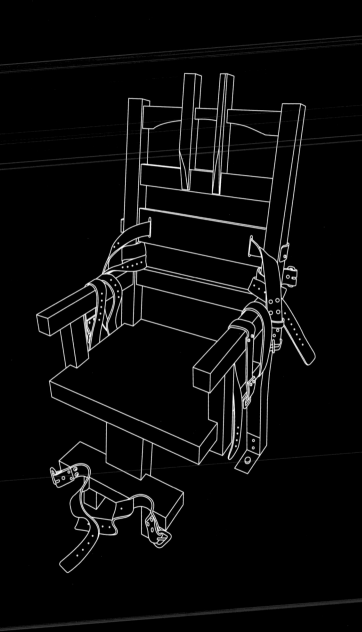

DEATH PENALTY THE FACTS

IN 2007, 88 PERCENT OF ALL KNOWN EXECUTIONS TOOK
PLACE IN FIVE COUNTRIES: CHINA, IRAN, SAUDI ARABIA,
PAKISTAN AND THE USA.

IN 2007 IRAN EXECUTED AT LEAST 317 PEOPLE,
SAUDI ARABIA 143 AND PAKISTAN 135.
THERE WERE 42 EXECUTIONS IN 10 STATES IN THE USA.

SAUDI ARABIA HAD THE HIGHEST NUMBER OF EXECUTIONS
PER CAPITA, FOLLOWED BY IRAN AND LIBYA.

TWO-THIRDS OF THE WORLD'S 785 MILLION ILLITERATE ADULTS ARE WOMEN

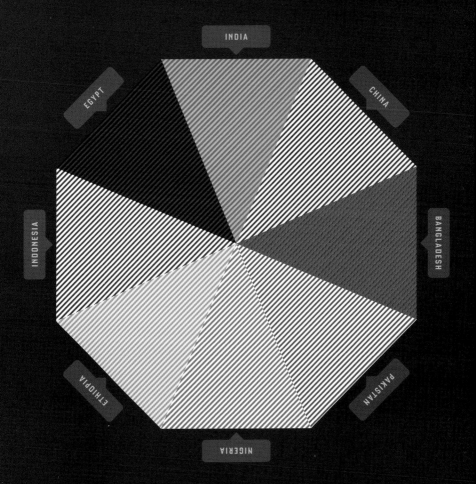

INDIA

CHINA

EGYPT

BANGLADESH

INDONESIA

ETHIOPIA

PAKISTAN

NIGERIA

TWO-THIRDS OF THE WORLD'S 785 MILLION ILLITERATE ADULTS ARE FOUND IN ONLY EIGHT COUNTRIES

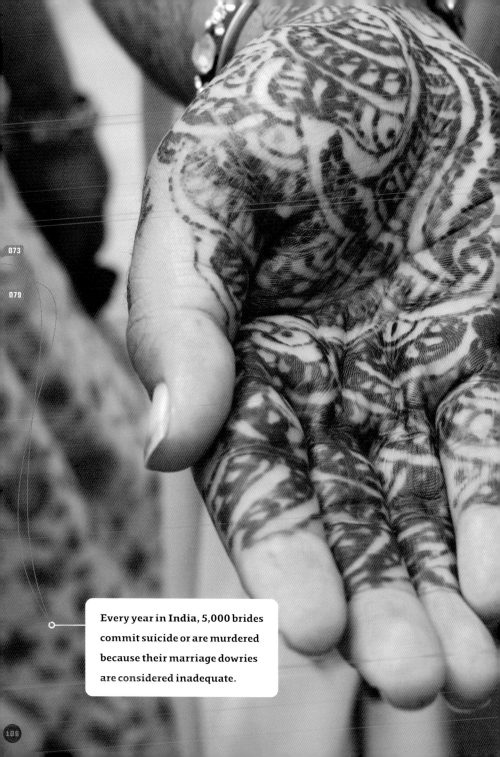

Every year in India, 5,000 brides commit suicide or are murdered because their marriage dowries are considered inadequate.

800,000

75%

75% OF VICTIMS ARE TRAFFICKED INTO
COMMERCIAL SEXUAL EXPLOITATION.

800,000 PEOPLE A YEAR ARE TRAFFICKED ACROSS NATIONAL BORDERS.

80% 50%

80% OF THE VICTIMS ARE FEMALE.

50% OF THE VICTIMS ARE MINORS.

LARGE NUMBERS OF REFUGEES FLEE
NORTH KOREA EVERY YEAR HAVING
SUFFERED FOOD SHORTAGES,
POLITICAL REPRESSION AND HUMAN
RIGHTS VIOLATIONS. MANY CROSS THE BORDER INTO CHINA WHERE THEY —
WOMEN ESPECIALLY — ARE VULNERABLE TO ABUSE OR TRAFFICKING.
WOMEN ARE TRAFFICKED BY MARRIAGE-BROKERS AND SOLD AS BRIDES
IN RURAL AREAS WHERE THERE IS A SHORTAGE OF MARRIAGE-AGE WOMEN
(OWING TO THE PREFERENCE FOR MALE-BABIES IN CHINA'S ONE CHILD SYSTEM).
A SURVEY CARRIED OUT BY HUMAN RIGHTS GROUP, THE U.S. COMMITTEE FOR
HUMAN RIGHTS IN NORTH KOREA, FOUND THE AVERAGE PRICE FOR A BRIDE
TO BE AROUND 1,900 RMB
(APPROXIMATELY $244), ALTHOUGH
MANY WERE SOLD FOR LESS THAN
1,700 RMB (APPROXIMATELY $218).

The Great Firewall Of China

Freedom And Democracy Forum / F

Armageddon / TOP TEN WOF

POLLUTION LAW

HIRE A KILLER TO MURDER ONE'S WIFE / **Sor**

Tiananmen Massacre / CHI

North Korea Falls Out With China / **NUCL**

HORSE RACING / *Quit the Par*

NO. 1 EVIL CULT IN T

112

s Riots / FETUS SOUP /

CITIES / Mascot /

UIT / Cat Abuse /

of High Officials /

E ORPHANAGE /

R BOMB / Tibet Independence /

Handmade pistol /

WORLD /

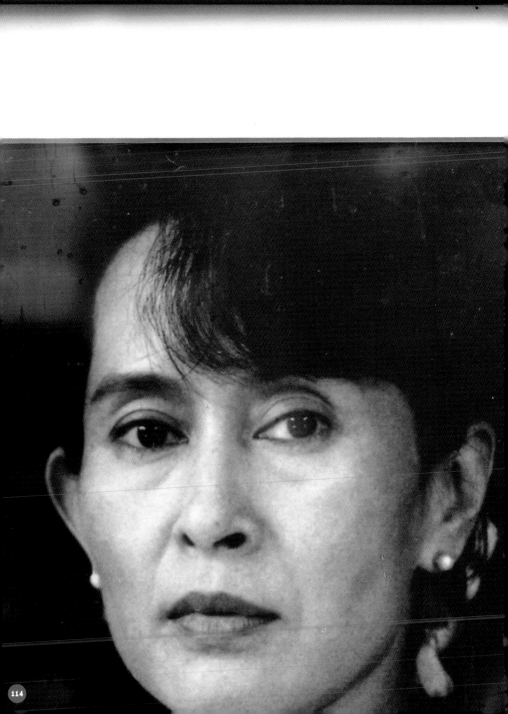

Aung San Suu Kyi

urma (Myanmar) has been ruled by military junta since 1962.
he regime has brutally suppressed almost all dissent and
ntinues to intimidate political activists and human rights
fenders. In 1990 the main opposition party, the National
ague for Democracy (NLD), won a landslide victory in
ational elections. However the junta refused to hand over
wer, instead placing the NLD leader and Nobel Peace Prize
cipient Aung San Suu Kyi under house arrest. Suu Kyi has
en held in this way for fourteen of the last twenty years,
able to speak to her party and supporters.

BETWEEN

1998 AND 2007

GLOBAL MILITARY SPENDING

INCREASED BY

45%

TOP MILITARY SPENDING COUNTRIES AND ARMS PRODUCING COMPANIES

The USA has a monopoly on the global arms market, spending 41.5% of the total expenditure and controlling six of the ten largest arms producing companies. China has recently become the second largest military spender for the first time, giving an indication of its growing global ambitions. The top five military spenders also happen to be the five permanent members of the United Nations Security Council.

MILITARY SPENDING (BILLION US$)

	00	100	200	300	400	500	600

USA
CHINA
FRANCE
UK
RUSSIA
GERMANY
JAPAN
ITALY
SAUDI ARABIA
INDIA
WESTERN EUROPE

THE TOP 10 MILITARY SPENDERS, 2008

ARMS SALES (BILLION US$)

	00	05	10	15	20	25	30

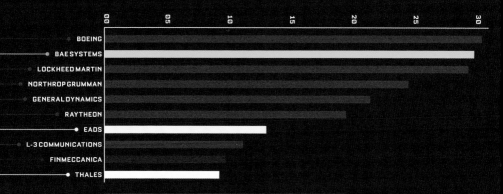

BOEING
BAE SYSTEMS
LOCKHEED MARTIN
NORTHROP GRUMMAN
GENERAL DYNAMICS
RAYTHEON
EADS
L-3 COMMUNICATIONS
FINMECCANICA
THALES

THE 10 LARGEST ARMS PRODUCING COMPANIES, 2007

121

ON FRIDAY 31 OCTOBER 2008, 147 STATES VOTED AT THE UNITED NATIONS
TO MOVE FORWARD WITH WORK ON AN ARMS TRADE TREATY.

ONLY THE USA AND ZIMBABWE VOTED AGAINST.

THE MERCHANT OF DEATH

Viktor Bout, a former Russian lieutenant, is alleged to be one of the world's biggest arms dealers. He earned the nickname 'the Merchant of Death' by illegally shipping arms to conflict zones around the world, whilst also reputedly working for the US government and the UN. When the USSR collapsed, Bout took advantage of the sudden availability of cheap Soviet planes and weapons, flying them around the world for any government or militia that would pay. His clients are believed to have ranged from Congolese warlords to the Taliban. Bout was arrested in 2008 whilst trying to procure weapons for FARC in Bangkok. The US is currently seeking Bout's extradition from Thailand.

EVERY YEAR
10 — 14 BILLION UNITS
OF SMALL ARMS AMMUNITIONS
ARE PRODUCED.
THAT'S TWO UNITS EACH
FOR EVERY PERSON
ON THE PLANET.

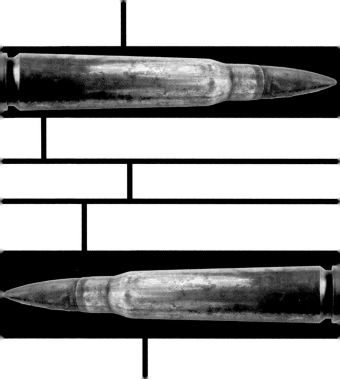

COLUMBIA HAS THE HIGHEST GUN HOMICIDE RATE IN THE WORLD, 495 TIMES HIGHER THAN THAT OF THE UK

GUN HOMICIDE RATES PER 100,000 PEOPLE PER YEAR:

THE TOP TEN

01.	COLUMBIA	49.52
02.	HONDURAS	30.57
03.	EL SALVADOR	22.46
04.	SOUTH AFRICA	22.40
05.	BRAZIL	21.07
06.	VENEZUELA	21.04
07.	GUATEMALA	17.10
08.	JAMAICA	16.97
09.	ECUADOR	10.16
10.	PHILIPPINES	9.64

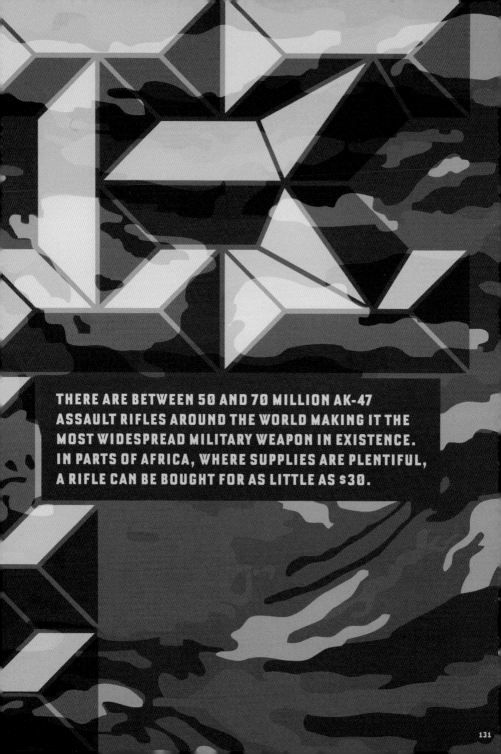

THERE ARE BETWEEN 50 AND 70 MILLION AK-47 ASSAULT RIFLES AROUND THE WORLD MAKING IT THE MOST WIDESPREAD MILITARY WEAPON IN EXISTENCE. IN PARTS OF AFRICA, WHERE SUPPLIES ARE PLENTIFUL, A RIFLE CAN BE BOUGHT FOR AS LITTLE AS $30.

The bomblets contained within one cluster bomb can cover an area the size of 8 soccer pitches.

In 2003, during three weeks of major combat in Iraq, the US and UK used nearly 13,000 cluster munitions, containing an estimated 1.8 to 2 million submunitions.

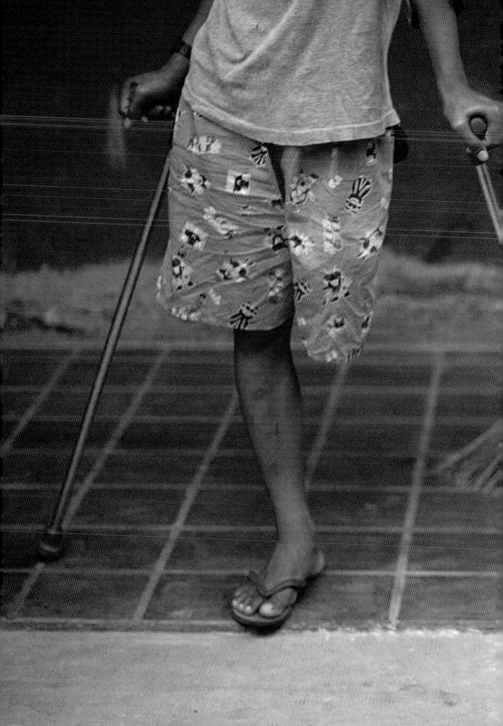

ONE LAND MINE CAN COST AS LITTLE AS $3 TO MAKE BUT $1000 TO DESTROY.

THERE ARE OVER TEN
THOUSAND DEPLOYED NUCLEAR
WARHEADS WORLDWIDE.

NINETY PERCENT OF THESE ARE
HELD BY JUST TWO COUNTRIES:
USA AND RUSSIA.

DURING WORLD WAR I, CIVILIAN CASUALTIES WERE LESS THAN 5 PERCENT

TODAY THE AMOUNT OF CIVILIANS KILLED OR WOUNDED IN WARS TOTAL 45 PERCENT

THE BITTER CIVIL WAR THAT HAS RAGED IN THE DEMOCRATIC REPUBLIC OF CONGO SINCE 1998 HAS CLAIMED THE LIVES OF OVER 5.4 MILLION PEOPLE, MAKING IT THE WORLD'S DEADLIEST CRISIS SINCE WORLD WAR II. HOWEVER JUST ONE PERCENT OF THESE DEATHS HAVE RESULTED FROM VIOLENCE, MOST ARE DUE TO A CHRONIC LACK OF MEDICAL CARE AS THE COUNTRY'S INFRASTRUCTURE HAS BEEN TORN APART BY THE CONFLICT.

THE FIGHT FOR CONTROL OF THE COUNTRY'S RICH MINERAL RESOURCES HAS SEEN GOVERNMENT FORCES, SUPPORTED BY ANGOLA, NAMIBIA AND ZIMBABWE, COMBATING REBELS BACKED BY UGANDA AND RWANDA. CIVILIANS HAVE BEEN MOST AFFECTED BY THE CONFLICT, WITH HUNDREDS OF THOUSANDS OF PEOPLE DISPLACED. CONDITIONS FOR WOMEN HAVE BEEN ESPECIALLY DIFFICULT WITH THOUSANDS OF REPORTED CASES OF RAPE AND SEXUAL ABUSE.

It took just 100 days for an estimated 800,000 Rwandans to be killed during the 1994 Rwandan genocide. Most of those killed were Tutsis; most of those who committed the violence were Hutus.

There are over two hundred and fifty thousand child soldiers involved in twenty conflict zones around the world.

1. **AFGHANISTAN**

2. **BURUNDI**

3. **CENTRAL AFRICAN REPUBLIC**

4. **CHAD**

5. **COLOMBIA**

6. **CÔTE D'IVOIRE**

7. **DEMOCRATIC REPUBLIC OF CONGO**

8. **GEORGIA**

9. **HAITI**

10. **IRAQ**

11. **LEBANON**

12. **MYANMAR**

13. **NEPAL**

14. **OCCUPIED PALESTINIAN TERRITORY/ISRAEL**

15. **THE PHILIPPINES**

16. **SOMALIA**

17. **SRI LANKA**

18. **SUDAN**

19. **THAILAND**

20. **UGANDA**

IN 2008 THERE WERE MORE THAN

100 PIRACY ATTACKS

INCLUDING 40 SUCCESSFUL HIJACKINGS

Somalia is a failed state and has been without
effective central government since 1991.
The country has been gripped in a vicious civil war
since then, leading to a humanitarian crisis with
a third of the population being dependant on food aid.

It is against this backdrop that there has been
a surge in piracy along the Somalian coast.
Ships are advised to keep more than 450 nautical
miles away from the coast as the pirates are heavily
armed with rocket-propelled grenades and AK-47s.

Piracy is a lucrative business, with the
Somalian pirates taking an estimated
$150m in ransom payments in 2008.

Between June 2007 and June 2009 IED explosions in Iraq decreased by 90%

Before that they were responsible for 50% of combat deaths

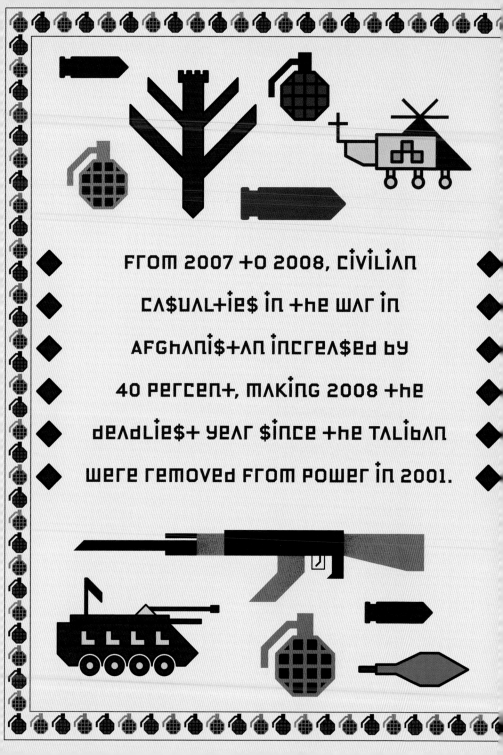

FROM 2007 TO 2008, CIVILIAN CASUALTIES IN THE WAR IN AFGHANISTAN INCREASED BY 40 PERCENT, MAKING 2008 THE DEADLIEST YEAR SINCE THE TALIBAN WERE REMOVED FROM POWER IN 2001.

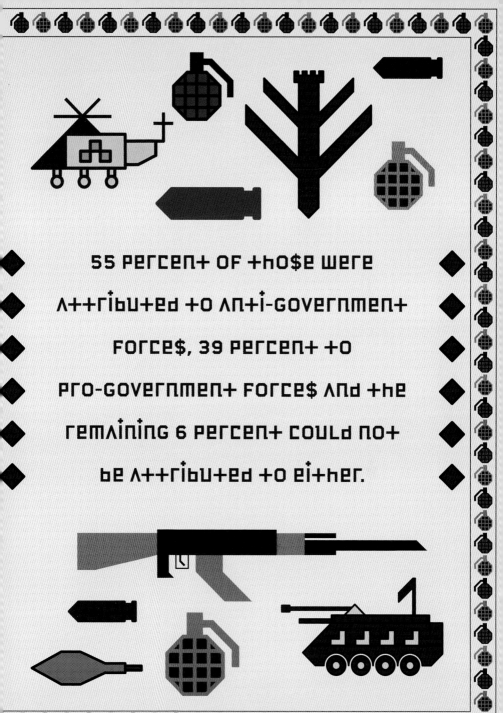

55 percent of those were attributed to anti-government forces, 39 percent to pro-government forces and the remaining 6 percent could not be attributed to either.

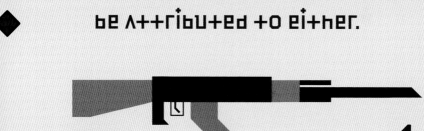

CONFLICT TYPES

INTRASTATE CONFLICT

INTERNATIONALISED INTRASTATE CONFLICT

INTERSTATE CONFLICT

In the past 60 years interstate conflicts (conflicts between two or more governments) have been by far the most deadly (34,677 people killed per year). Intrastate conflicts (conflict between a government and a non-governmental party, with no interference from other countries) have been the most common, yet the least deadly. The wars in Iraq and Afghanistan are considered to be internationalised intrastate conflicts, that is — they are conflicts that take place within one country but involve foreign military forces.

In January 2009 Israel launched a series of air strikes aimed at the Gaza Strip, in an attempt to stop Hamas from firing rockets into towns and villages in southern Israel. During the three-week conflict, 1,400 Palestinians were killed – including 300 children – and a further 5,000 were wounded. Three Israeli civilians were killed.

In this period, Israel also damaged or destroyed 48% of the health facilities in Gaza. This breaks down as:

15 hospitals and 41 primary healthcare centres partially damaged;

2 primary healthcare centres destroyed;

29 ambulances partially damaged or destroyed.

Between 1990 and 2007,
negotiations led to the end of
59 conflicts around the world.
In those 17 years, military
victories resulted in the end of
only 27 conflicts. This has become
the first period in recorded history
where more conflicts have ended
in negotiation than in violence.

Illicit Drugs

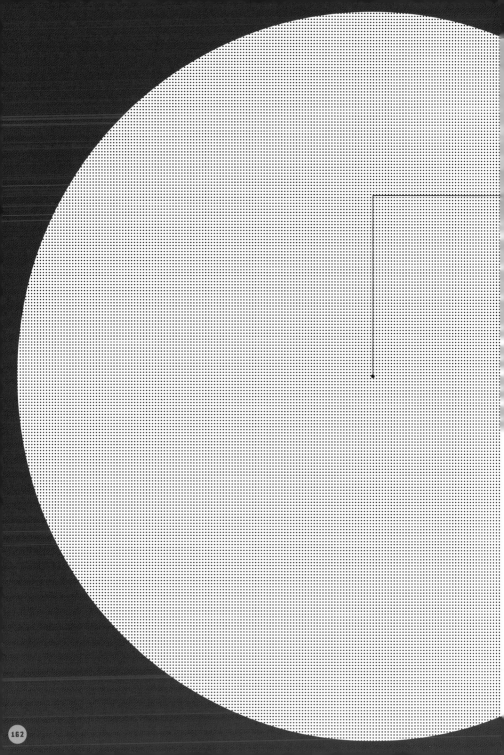

$322 RETAIL

$94 WHOLESALE

$13 PRODUCTION

As illegal drugs move through the supply chain from producer to consumer they increase in value by a staggering 2,477 percent – despite seizures and losses suffered along the way.

HONG KONG

On 1 July 1997, Hong Kong became a Special Administrative Region of the People's Republic of China, having been occupied by the UK since 1841. Following the defeat of the Chinese during the first Opium War, it was signed over to the British under the treaty of Nanking. The war had been fought after the Qing dynasty banned the British East India Company from importing opium into China. The subsequent smuggling; arrests; second Opium War; burning of the Imperial Summer Palace; and forced importation ultimately led to the legalisation of domestic opium production in China. Production steadily increased until 1890 when it rocketed to thirty-five thousand metric tons per year – this dwarfs today's global output of just 8,000 metric tons. At the end of the 18th century, Chinese opium addiction reached epidemic proportions and was the greatest drug abuse problem the world had ever faced.

178

094

152

155

90% **OF THE WORLD'S**
OPIUM

+ × × + × × + × × + × × + × × + × × + × × + × × + × × + × × + × × + × × +

— I S   P R O D U C E D   B Y —

[ΔFGHΔNI⊃+ΔN]

+ × × + × × + × × + × × + × × + × × + × × + × × + × × + × × + × × + × × +

YET LESS **2%** OF IT IS
THAN SEIZED THERE

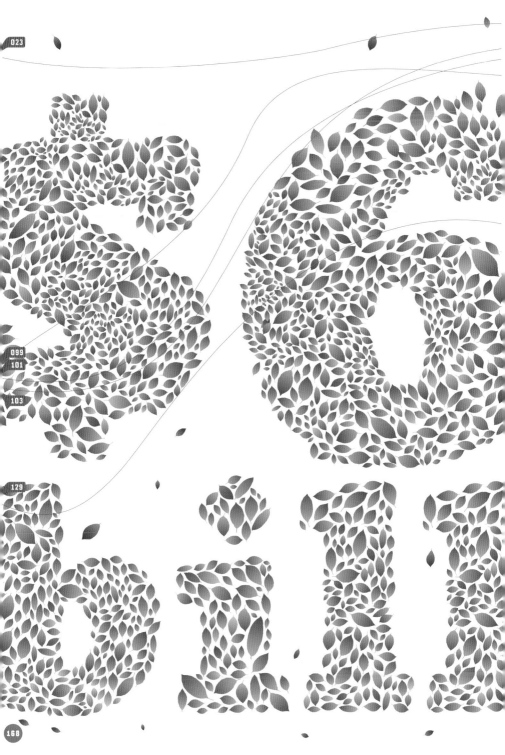
023
099
101
103
129

Since 2000 the **United States** has sent over $6 billion dollars worth of aid to **Columbia** as part of Plan Columbia, a $7.5 billion multi-year strategy aimed at tackling Columbia's drug problem. The majority of the money has been pumped into the military and police, with some being put into alternative development schemes. However despite such huge resources and a plan to cut cocaine production in half by 2006, production hit a record high in 2005. Columbia continues to be the world's largest producer of cocaine (51%) followed by Peru (36%) and **Bolivia** (13%).

IN 2008 THE GLOBAL STREET VALUE FOR A GRAM OF COCAINE RANGED BETWEEN $89 AND $200.

IN BOLIVIA, THE AVERAGE FARM-GATE PRICE FOR A KILOGRAM OF COCA LEAVES (THE RAW INGREDIENT FOR COCAINE) WAS $5.50.

Morocco is
the world's largest
cannabis resin producer,
primarily supplying the
European market.

There are
around 89,000 households
and 760,000 people
involved in the cultivation
of cannabis.

The value of
trade in Moroccan
originated cannabis resin
is estimated to be around
$5.5 billion per year.

Each
household earns an
average annual
income of $4,300.

The Soupmaker

Mexico has been gripped in a brutal drug war since 2006, when President Felipe Calderón declared war on the drug cartels. Since then there have been thousands of drug-related killings, gun battles, assassinations and kidnappings. There have, however, probably been few stranger stories than 'The Soupmaker'. Whilst working for a powerful drug trafficking cartel, hit man Santiago Meza Lopez disposed of three hundred bodies over ten years. He did this by dumping the remains in acid, being paid just $600 a week for his work.

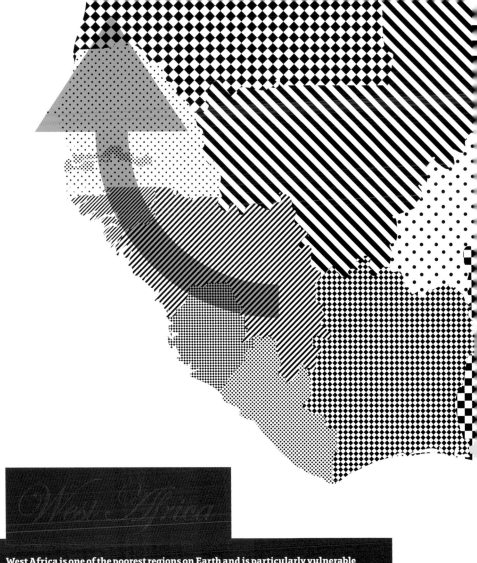

West Africa

West Africa is one of the poorest regions on Earth and is particularly vulnerable to organised crime due to its weak governance. Between 1998 and 2007 West Africa experienced a startlingly rapid rise in cocaine trafficking, with seizures increasing seven-fold in that period. The estimated value of the flow during this time was almost two billion dollars. It has now decreased to a flow of around one billion dollars per anum due to the international focus on the area. It is clear that corruption was endemic in the region, with high profile figures such as the son of the President of Guinea confessing involvement in trafficking.

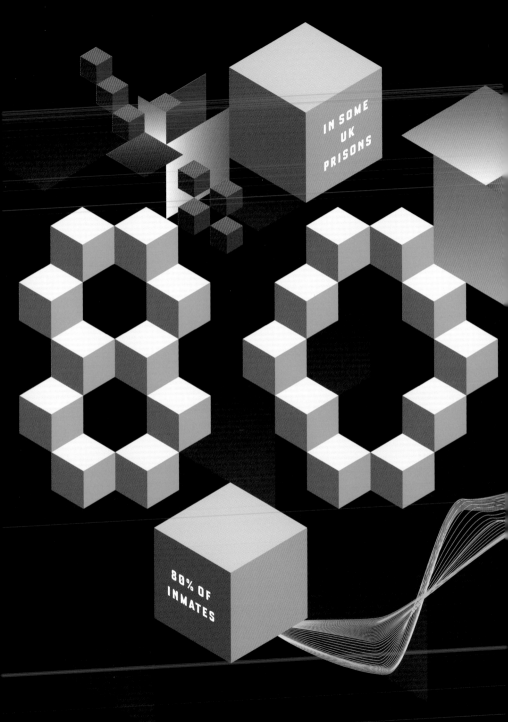

IN SOME
UK
PRISONS

80% OF
INMATES

ON A
GLOBAL SCALE,
500 METRIC TONS OF
ATS (AMPHETAMINE-TYPE
STIMULANTS) ARE PRODUCED
ANNUALLY, WITH A TOTAL
MARKET VALUE OF AROUND
$65 BILLION.

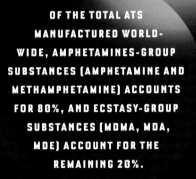

OF THE TOTAL ATS
MANUFACTURED WORLD-
WIDE, AMPHETAMINES-GROUP
SUBSTANCES (AMPHETAMINE AND
METHAMPHETAMINE) ACCOUNTS
FOR 80%, AND ECSTASY-GROUP
SUBSTANCES (MDMA, MDA,
MDE) ACCOUNT FOR THE
REMAINING 20%.

ATS ARE ATTRACTIVE
TO PRODUCERS AS THEY
REQUIRE LITTLE INVESTMENT,
AND CAN MANUFACTURED FROM
A NUMBER OF STARTING MATERIALS.
THEY ARE HIGHLY PROFITABLE;
THE MARK-UP FROM WHOLESALE
TO RETAIL LEVEL CAN BE AS
MUCH AS 400%.

SOURCES/BIBLIOGRAPHY

P.10 | WEALTH DISTRIBUTION
The World Trade System
September 2003 | Friends of the Earth International
http://www.foei.org/en/publications/pdfs/worldtradesystem.pdf

P.12 | DISPROPORTIONATE TARIFFS
Trade and Livelihoods
Oxfam
http://www.oxfam.org.uk/resources/issues/trade/introduction.html

P.14 | TRADE RESTRICTIONS
Rigged Rules and Double Standards
Kevin Watkins, Penny Fowler | 2002 | Make Trade Fair (Oxfam) |
ISBN-10 0855985259
http://www.oxfam.org.uk/what_we_do/issues/trade/downloads/trade_report.pdf

P.16 | UNFAIR TRADE KENYA
Why More Free Trade Won't Help Africa
September 2005 | Traidcraft Policy Unit
http://www.traidcraft.co.uk/OneStopCMS/Core/CrawlerResourceServer.
aspx?resource=53BD19CC-07A8-4084-884C-2CE57BBB0F9D6mode=link&guid
=d593a3c6ef68486f8c6758269e7d84c4f

P.18 | SHELL NIGERIA
Shell settles Nigeria deaths case
June 2009 | BBC News
http://news.bbc.co.uk/1/hi/world/africa/8090493.stm
—
Case Study: Shell
Friends of the Earth
http://www.foe.co.uk/campaigns/economy/case_studies/shell_index.html

P.20 | CREDIT CRUNCH FOR DEVELOPING COUNTRIES
Global Monitoring Report 2009
2009 | The International Bank for Reconstruction and Development /
The World Bank | ISBN 978-0-8213-7859-5
http://siteresources.worldbank.org/INTGLOMONREP2009/
Resources/5924349-1239742507025/GMR09_book.pdf

P.22 | WHO CONTROLS THE WORLD BANK
Challenging Corporate Investor Rule
Sarah Anderson and Sara Grusky | April 2007 |
Institute for Policy Studies and Food and Water Watch
www.ips-dc.org/reports/070430-challengingcorporateinvestorrule.pdf

P.24 | GHANA
Trade Issue 109 | The Tyranny of Free Trade
December 2005 | Friends of the Earth | ISBN 90-0914913-9
http://www.foe.org.au/resources/publications/trade-and-globalisation/
tyranny.pdf

P.26 | WEALTH/CONFLICT
Investing in Development
2005 | United Nations Development Programme
http://www.unmillenniumproject.org/documents/overviewEngLowRes.pdf

P.28 | ZIMBABWE HYPER-INFLATION
Zimbabwe rolls out Z$100tr note
January 2009 | BBC News
http://news.bbc.co.uk/2/hi/africa/7832601.stm

P.32 | DEFORESTATION
Deforestation causes global warming
September 2006 | The Food and Agriculture Organization
of the United Nations
http://www.fao.org/newsroom/en/news/2006/1000385/index.html
—
Global Forest Resources Assessment 2005
2006 | The Food and Agriculture Organization of the United Nations
ftp://ftp.fao.org/docrep/fao/008/A0400E/A0400E00.pdf
—
FRA 2005 Global tables
2005 | The Food and Agriculture Organization of the United Nations
www.fao.org/forestry/static/data/fra2005/global_tables/
FRA_2005_Global_Tables_EN.xls

P.34 | DEFORESTATION BRAZIL
FRA 2005 Global tables
2005 | The Food and Agriculture Organization of the United Nations
www.fao.org/forestry/static/data/fra2005/global_tables/
FRA_2005_Global_Tables_EN.xls
—
Amazon Cattle Footprint
29 January 2009 | Greenpeace Brazil
http://www.greenpeace.org/raw/content/international/press/reports/
amazon-cattle-footprint-mato.pdf

SOURCES/BIBLIOGRAPHY

P.36 | CHINA AIR QUALITY

Cost of Pollution in China
February 2007 | World Bank | Environmental and Social
Development Unit East Asia & Pacific Region
siteresources.worldbank.org/INTEAPREGTOPENVIRONMENT/Resources/
China_Cost_of_Pollution.pdf

P.38 | CHINA THREE GORGES

Three Gorges dam: the Cost of Power
October 2008 | International Rivers
http://www.internationalrivers.org/files/3Gorges_factsheet.lorez_.pdf

—

Three Gorges dam wall completed
May 2006 | BBC News
http://news.bbc.co.uk/1/hi/world/asia-pacific/5000092.st

P.40 | TOP 20 CARBON EMMITTING COUNTRIES

**H.1co2 World Carbon Dioxide Emissions from the
Consumption and Flaring of Fossil Fuels, 1980–2006**
2006 | International Energy Annual 2006 |
Energy Information Administration
http://www.eia.doe.gov/pub/international/iealf/tableh1co2.xls

P.42 | WORLD BANK CARBON FOOTPRINT

The World Bank and its carbon footprint
Lies Craeynest and Daisy Streatfeild | 23 June 2008 | WWF
http://www.wwf.org.uk/filelibrary/pdf/world_bank_report.pdf

P.44 | NUCLEAR POWER

Nuclear power – the problems
Greenpeace
http://www.greenpeace.org.uk/nuclear/problems

P.46 | CHERNOBYL

Chernobyl FAQ
International Atomic Energy Agency
http://www.iaea.org/NewsCenter/Features/Chernobyl-15/cherno-faq.shtml

—

**Chernobyl's Legacy: Health, Environmental
and Socio-Economic Impacts**
2005 | The Chernobyl Forum: 2003–2005 |
International Atomic Energy Agency
http://www.iaea.org/Publications/Booklets/Chernobyl/chernobyl.pdf

P.48 – P.51 | EFFECTS OF GLOBAL WARMING

**Climate calendar The UK's unjust contribution
to global climate change**
Tim Jones and Peter Hardstaff | January 2007 |
World Development Movement
http://www.wdm.org.uk/sites/default/files/climatecalandarreport08012007.pdf

P.54 | TOBACCO USE

World Health Statistics 2008
2008 | World Health Organisation | ISBN 978-92-4-0682740
www.who.int/whosis/whostat/EN_WHS08_Full.pdf

P.56 | MALARIA

Fast Facts: The Faces of Poverty
UN Millennium Project
www.unmillenniumproject.org/documents/UNMP-FastFacts-E.pdf

P.58 | HIV/AIDS

Fast Facts: The Faces of Poverty
UN Millennium Project
www.unmillenniumproject.org/documents/UNMP-FastFacts-E.pdf

P.60 | HIV/AIDS SWAZILAND

Swaziland
December 2005 | World Health Organisation
www.who.int/hiv/HIVCP_SWZ.pdf

P.62 | THE US PHARMACEUTICAL INDUSTRY

**The Cost of Pushing Pills: A New Estimate
of Pharmaceutical Promotion Expenditures
in the United States**
Marc-André Gagnon & Joel Lexchin | January 2008 |
PLoS Medicine, Volume 5, Issue 1
http://www.plosmedicine.org/article/fetchObjectAttachment.action;jsessionid
=4ECF5A25B0248698088B189C32B07B42?uri=info%3Adoi%2F10.1371%2Fjour
nal.pmed.0050001&representation=PDF

P.64 | MALNOURISHED/OVERWEIGHT

Number of undernourished persons
August 2008 | FAO Statistics Division
http://www.fao.org/fileadmin/templates/ess/documents/
food_security_statistics/NumberUndernourishment_en.xls

SOURCES/BIBLIOGRAPHY

P.64 | MALNOURISHED/OVERWEIGHT

Fact sheet 311 | Obesity and overweight
September 2006 | World Health Organisation
http://www.who.int/mediacentre/factsheets/fs311/en/index.html

P.66 | WORLD WATER FACTS

Fast Facts: The Faces of Poverty
UN Millennium Project
www.unmillenniumproject.org/documents/UNMP-FastFacts-E.pdf
—
Human Development Report 2006
United Nations Development Programme | ISBN 0-230-50058-7
hdr.undp.org/en/media/HDR06-complete.pdf

P.68 | ZIMBABWE'S CHOLERA OUTBREAK

Zimbabwe cholera 'past its peak'
March 2009 | BBC News
http://news.bbc.co.uk/1/hi/world/africa/7960674.stm

P.70 | CHILDBIRTH

Fast Facts: The Faces of Poverty
UN Millennium Project
www.unmillenniumproject.org/documents/UNMP-FastFacts-E.pdf
—
World Health Statistics 2008
2008 | World Health Organisation| ISBN 978-92-4-0682740
www.who.int/whosis/whostat/EN_WHS08_Full.pdf

P.72 | ORGAN TRANSPLANT TRADE

The State of the International Organ Trade:
A Provisional Picture Based on Integration
of Available Information
Yosuke Shimazono | December 2007 | Bulletin of the World Health
Organization | Volume 85, Number 12, 901-980
http://www.who.int/bulletin/volumes/85/12/06-039370/en/
—
The State of the International Organ Trade:
A Provisional Picture Based on Integration
of Available Information
Yosuke Shimazono | December 2007 | Table 1. Transplant tourism
web sites available 21 March 2007 | Bulletin of the World Health
Organization | Volume 85, Number 12, 955-962
http://www.who.int/bulletin/volumes/85/12/06-039370-table-T1.html

P.76 | POPULATION GROWTH

World Population Prospects | The 2008 Revision
2009 | Department of Economic and Social Affairs |
United Nations Population Division
http://www.un.org/esa/population/publications/wpp2008/
wpp2008_highlights.pdf

P.78 | POPULATION DISTRIBUTION

World Population Prospects | The 2008 Revision
2009 | Department of Economic and Social Affairs |
United Nations Population Division
http://www.un.org/esa/population/publications/wpp2008/
wpp2008_highlights.pdf

P.80 | NIGER

Africa : Niger
2009 | CIA World Factbook
https://www.cia.gov/library/publications/the-world-factbook/geos/ng.html

P.82 | URBAN POPULATION

Urban Population, Development
and the Environment 2007
March 2008 | United Nations Population Division |
ISBN 978-92-1-151443-8-1
http://www.un.org/esa/population/publications/2007_PopDevt/
Urban_2007.pdf
—
Urban Agglomerations 2007
June 2008 | United Nations Population Division |
ISBN 978-92-1-151447-6
http://www.un.org/esa/population/publications/wup2007/
2007_urban_agglomerations_chart.pdf

P.84 | TOKYO

An Overview of Urbanization, Internal Migration,
Population Distribution and Development
in the World
January 2008 | United Nations Population Division |
UN/POP/EGM-URB/2008/01
http://www.un.org/esa/population/meetings/EGM_PopDist/P01_UNPopDiv.pdf

SOURCES/BIBLIOGRAPHY

P.86 | SLUM POPULATION

What Are Slums and Why Do They Exist?
April 2007 | UN-HABITAT | GRHS/03/B5
http://www.unhabitat.org/downloads/docs/
4625_51419_GC%2021%20What%20are%20slums.pdf

—

**Urban Population, Development
and the Environment 2007**
March 2008 | United Nations Population Division |
ISBN 978-92-1-151443-8-1
http://www.un.org/esa/population/publications/2007_PopDevt/
Urban_2007.pdf

P.88 | KIBERA SLUM

Facts & Information About Kibera
2007 | Kibera UK
http://www.kibera.org.uk/Facts.html

P.90 | PEOPLE OF CONCERN

**2008 Global Trends: Refugees, Asylum-seekers,
Returnees, Internally Displaced and
Stateless Persons**
June 2009 | UNHCR
http://www.unhcr.org/4a375c426.html

P.92 | THE MYTH OF REFUGEES

**2007 Global Trends: Refugees, Asylum-seekers,
Returnees, Internally Displaced and
Stateless Persons**
June 2008 | UNHCR
http://www.unhcr.org/statistics/STATISTICS/4852366f2.pdf

P.94 | AFGHANISTAN'S REFUGEE CRISIS

**2008 Global Trends: Refugees, Asylum-seekers,
Returnees, Internally Displaced and
Stateless Persons**
June 2009 | UNHCR
http://www.unhcr.org/4a375c426.html

P.98 | PRISON POPULATIONS

World Prison Population List (fourth edition)
2003 | Home Office | ISSN 1473-8406
www.homeoffice.gov.uk/rds/pdfs2/r188.pdf

P.100 | GUANTANAMO

Facts and Figures | Illegal US Detentions
December 2008 | Amnesty International |
AI Index: AMR 51/147/2008
http://www.amnesty.org.au/images/uploads/hrs/facts_and_figures.pdf

P.102 | DEATH PENALTY

**Death penalty: Death sentences
and executions in 2007**
April 2008 | Amnesty International | AI Index: ACT 50/001/2008
http://www.amnesty.org/en/library/asset/ACT50/001/2008/en/b43a1e5b-
ffea-11dc-b092-bdb020617d3d/act500012008eng.pdf

P.104 | ILLITERACY

**WHO Report on the Global Tobacco Epidemic,
2008: the MPOWER package.**
2008 | World Health Organization | ISBN 978-92-4159628-2
www.who.int/tobacco/mpower/mpower_report_full_2008.pdf

P.106 | DOWRIES INDIA

Gender Violence Facts and Figures
2009 | Women's Learning Partnership
http://learningpartnership.org/en/resources/facts/violence

P.108 | TRAFFICKING IN PERSONS

World / Transnational Issues / Trafficking in persons
2009 | CIA World Factbook
https://www.cia.gov/library/publications/the-world-factbook/geos/xx.html

P.110 | PRICE OF NORTH KOREAN BRIDES IN CHINA

**The North Korean Refugee Crisis:
Human Rights and International Response**
Stephan Haggard and Marcus Noland | 2006 | U.S. Committee
for Human Rights in North Korea | ISBN 0-9771-1111-3
http://www.hrnk.org/refugeesReport06.pdf

P.112 | GREAT FIREWALL OF CHINA

Keywords Used to Filter Web Content
February 2006 | The Washington Post
http://www.washingtonpost.com/wp-dyn/content/article/2006/02/18/
AR2006021800554.html

SOURCES/BIBLIOGRAPHY

P.114 | AUNG SAN SUU KYI
World Report 2009
2009 | Human Rights Watch | ISBN-13 978-1-58322-858-6
www.hrw.org/sites/default/files/reports/wr2009_web.pdf
—

CIA World Factbook / Burma
2009 | CIA World Factbook
https://www.cia.gov/library/publications/the-world-factbook/geos/bm.html

P.118 | MILITARY SPENDING
Recent Trends in The Arms Trade
Mark Bromley, Paul Holtom, Sam Perlo-Freeman,
Pieter D. Wezeman | April 2009 | SIPRI
http://books.sipri.org/files/misc/SIPRIBP0904a.pdf

P.120 | TOP ARMS PRODUCERS
SIPRI Yearbook 2009:
Armaments, Disarmament and International Security
June 2009 | SIPRI | ISBN 978-0-19-956606-8
http://www.sipri.org/yearbook/2009/files/SIPRIYB09summary.pdf

P.122 | ARMS TRADE TREATY VOTE
Landslide UN vote in favor of Arms Trade Treaty
October 2008 | Oxfam press release
http://www.oxfam.org/en/pressroom/pressrelease/2008-10-31/
landslide-un-vote-favor-arms-trade-treaty

P.124 | VIKTOR BOUT
Profile: Viktor Bout
March 2008 | BBC News
http://news.bbc.co.uk/1/hi/7281885.stm
—

'Merchant of Death' denies arming terror
Nick Paton Walsh | March 2009 | The Observer
http://www.guardian.co.uk/world/2009/mar/15/
viktor-bout-merchant-of-death

P.126 | SMALL ARMS AMMUNITIONS
Killer Facts
Control Arms
http://www.controlarms.org/en/documents%20and%20files/killer-facts2/view

P.128 | GUN HOMICIDE COLUMBIA
Gun Violence: The Global Crisis
2007 | International Action Network on Small Arms (IANSA)
http://www.iansa.org/un/documents/GlobalCrisis07.pdf

P.130 | AK-47
The Ak-47: The World's Favourite Killing Machine
June 2006 | Control Arms Briefing Note
http://www.controlarms.org/en/documents%20and%20files/reports/
english-reports/the-ak-47-the-worlds-favourite-weapon/view

P.132 | CLUSTER BOMBS
Military Fact Files / Cluster Bombs
2001 | BBC News
http://news.bbc.co.uk/hi/english/static/in_depth/world/2001/
cluster_bomb/5.stm
—

Cluster Munition Information Chart
August 2009 | Human Rights Watch
http://www.hrw.org/sites/default/files/related_material/2009.8.21%20
Arms%20Cluster%20Info%20Chart%20Updated.pdf

P.134 | LAND MINES
Landmine Contamination: A Development Imperative
Ian Bannon & Earl Turcotte | October 2004 |
UNDP Mine Action/World Bank
www.mineaction.org/CTA2/Landmine%20Contamination%20-%20A%20
Development%20Imperative.pdf

P.136 | NUCLEAR WEAPONS
SIPRI Yearbook 2009: Armaments,
Disarmament and International Security
June 2009 | ISBN 978-0-19-956606-8
http://www.sipri.org/yearbook/2009/files/SIPRIYB09summary.pdf

P.140 | CIVILIAN CASUALTIES
Did You Know?
Global Strategy Institute
http://gsi.csis.org/index.php?option=com_content&task=blogcategory&id=7
8&Itemid=113

P.142 | DRC
Congo's silent harvest of death
Mark Doyle | August 2008 | BBC News
http://news.bbc.co.uk/1/hi/world/africa/7554195.stm

SOURCES/BIBLIOGRAPHY

P.142 | DRC
Q&A: DR Congo conflict
January 2009 | BBC News
http://news.bbc.co.uk/1/hi/world/africa/3075537.stm

P.142 | DRC
Country profile: Democratic Republic of Congo
October 2009 | BBC News
http://news.bbc.co.uk/1/hi/world/africa/country_profiles/1076399.stm

P.144 | RWANDA
Rwanda: How the genocide happened
December 2008 | BBC News
http://news.bbc.co.uk/1/hi/world/africa/1288230.stm

P.146 | CHILD SOLDIERS
Situations of concern
March 2009 | Office of the Special Representative
of the Secretary-General for Children and Armed conflict
http://www.un.org/children/conflict/english/conflicts.html

P.148 | SOMALI PIRATES
Somalia's pirates seize 33 tanks
September 2008 | BBC News
http://news.bbc.co.uk/1/hi/world/africa/7637257.stm
—
Q&A: Somali piracy
January 2009 | BBC News
http://news.bbc.co.uk/1/hi/world/africa/7734985.stm

P.150 | IRAQ IEDS
Factsheet: Iraq Key Statistics, July 1, 2009
June 2009 | Institute for the Study of War
http://www.understandingwar.org/press-media/commentary/
factsheet-iraq-key-statistics-july-1-2009

P.152 | AFGHANISTAN CIVILIAN CASUALTIES
Number of Afghan civilian deaths in 2008
highest since Taliban ousted, says UN
February 2009 | UN News Centre
http://www.un.org/apps//news/story.asp?NewsID=29918&Cr=Afghan&Cr1=c
ivilian+rights

P.154 | DEATH BY TYPE OF CONFLICT
Human Security Brief 2007
Andrew Mack and Zoe Nielsen | 2007 | The Human Security
Report Project | Simon Fraser University, Canada
http://www.humansecuritybrief.info/HSRP_Brief_2007.pdf

P.156 | GAZA HEALTH FACILITIES
Amnesty International Report 2009 |
The State of the World's Human Rights
Amnesty International Publications | 2009 |
ISBN 978-0-86210-444-3
http://www.humansecuritybrief.info/HSRP_Brief_2007.pdf

P.158 | NEGOTIATIONS
Human Security Brief 2007
Andrew Mack and Zoe Nielsen | 2007 | The Human Security
Report Project | Simon Fraser University, Canada
http://www.humansecuritybrief.info/HSRP_Brief_2007.pdf

P.162 | TOTAL VALUE OF DRUGS TRADE
World Drug Report 2005
2005 | United Nations Office on Drugs and Crime (UNODC) |
ISBN 92-1-148200-3
http://www.unodc.org/pdf/WDR_2005/volume_1_web.pdf

P.164 | OPIUM WARS HONG KONG
World Drug Report 2008
2008 | United Nations Office on Drugs and Crime (UNODC) |
ISBN 978-92-1-148229-4
http://www.unodc.org/documents/wdr/WDR_2008/WDR_2008_eng_web.pdf

P.166 | OPIATE PRODUCTION AFGHANISTAN
Afghan Opium Market Plummets, says UNODC
September 2009 | United Nations Office
on Drugs and Crime (UNODC)
http://www.unodc.org/unodc/en/press/releases/2009/September/
afghan-opium-market-plummets-says-unodc.html

SOURCES/BIBLIOGRAPHY

P.166 | OPIATE PRODUCTION AFGHANISTAN

Afghanistan Opium Survey 2009
2009 | United Nations Office on Drugs and Crime (UNODC)
http://www.unodc.org/documents/crop-monitoring/Afghanistan/
Afghanistan_opium_survey_2009_summary.pdf

P.168 | PLAN COLOMBIA

World Drug Report 2009
2009 | United Nations Office on Drugs and Crime (UNODC) |
ISBN 978-92-1-148240-9
www.unodc.org/documents/wdr/WDR_2009/WDR2009_eng_web.pdf
—

Colombia
USAID Website
http://www.usaid.gov/pubs/cbj2002/lac/co/
—

The Truth About Plan Colombia
Adam B. Kushner | January 2009 | NEWSWEEK
http://www.newsweek.com/id/177681

P.170 | COCAINE FARMER PRICES

World Drug Report 2009
2009 | United Nations Office on Drugs and Crime (UNODC) |
ISBN 978-92-1-148240-9
www.unodc.org/documents/wdr/WDR_2009/WDR2009_eng_web.pdf

P.172 | CANNABIS PRODUCTION MOROCCO

Morocco Cannabis Survey 2005
2005 | United Nations Office on Drugs and Crime (UNODC)
http://www.unodc.org/pdf/research/Morocco_survey_2005_ex_sum.pdf

P.174 | THE SOUPMAKER

Mexican hit man dissolved 300 bodies in acid
January 2009 | The Daily Telegraph
http://www.telegraph.co.uk/news/worldnews/centralamericaandthecaribbean/
mexico/4343454/Mexican-hit-man-dissolved-300-bodies-in-acid.html

P.176 | TRAFFICKING

**Transnational Trafficking and the Rule of Law
in West Africa: A Threat Assessment**
July 2009 | United Nations Office on Drugs and Crime (UNODC)
http://www.unodc.org/documents/data-and-analysis/Studies/
West_Africa_Report_2009.pdf

P.176 | TRAFFICKING

World Drug Report 2009
2009 | United Nations Office on Drugs and Crime (UNODC) |
ISBN 978-92-1-148240-9
www.unodc.org/documents/wdr/WDR_2009/WDR2009_eng_web.pdf

P.176 | TRAFFICKING

Drug Trafficking as a Security Threat in West Africa
November 2008 | United Nations Office on Drugs and Crime (UNODC)
http://www.unodc.org/documents/data-and-analysis/Studies/
Drug-Trafficking-WestAfrica-English.pdf

P.178 | PRISON DRUG PROBLEM

The Prison Service Drug Strategy
November 2003 | HM Prison Service | Drug Strategy Unit
http://www.hmprisonservice.gov.uk/assets/documents/
10000157drugstrategyGenBriefingNote171203.doc

P.180 | ATS

Global ATS Assessment
2008 | United Nations Office on Drugs and Crime (UNODC)
http://www.unodc.org/documents/scientific/ATS/
Global-ATS-Assessment-Exec-summary.pdf

IMAGE CREDITS

FIELL

Published by Fiell Publishing Limited
www.fiell.com

A catalogue record for this book is available from the British Library
ISBN 978-1-906863-06-7

Note: The publisher has endeavored to ensure that the information
contained in this book was correct at the time of going to press.

Project Concept: Charlotte & Peter Fiell
Project Management: Charlotte Fiell
Art Direction, Design, Picture Sourcing, Research:
Jonathan Abbott at Barnbrook Design
Written by: Jonathan Abbott
Research: Steph Gillies and Nicola Ryan
Creative Direction: Jonathan Barnbrook

Printed in Hong Kong